MARTIN LUTHER KING JR. DAY

BY LINDA LOWERY
ILLUSTRATIONS BY HETTY MITCHELL

On My Own

HOLIDAYS

Revised Edition

Carolrhoda Books, Inc./Minneapolis

Thanks to the following for permission to reprint quotations in this book: Harper & Row, Publishers, Inc. for quote reprinted on page 21 from *Strive Toward Freedom: The Montgomery Story* by Martin Luther King Jr. Copyright © 1958 by Martin Luther King Jr. Reprinted by permission of Harper & Row, Publishers, Inc./Joan Daves for quote reprinted on page 42 from "I Have a Dream" by Martin Luther King Jr. Copyright © 1963 by Martin Luther King Jr. Reprinted by permission of Joan Daves/Detroit Free Press, Inc. for quotations by Mrs. Rosa Parks and Mrs. Coretta Scott King reprinted on page 56 from the "Living the Dream" supplement, *Detroit Free Press*, January 14, 1986.

This book is available in two editions:
Library binding by Carolrhoda Books, Inc., a division of Lerner Publishing Group
Soft cover by First Avenue Editions, an imprint of Lerner Publishing Group
241 First Avenue North
Minneapolis, Minnesota 55401 U.S.A.

Website address: www.lernerbooks.com

Library of Congress Cataloging-in-Publication Data

Lowery, Linda.
    Martin Luther King Jr. Day / by Linda Lowery ; illustrations by Hetty Mitchell.— Rev. ed.
        p.   cm. — (On my own holidays)
    Rev. ed. of: Martin Luther King Day. © 1987.
    Summary: Introduces Martin Luther King Jr. and relates how and why his birthday came to be celebrated as a national holiday.
    ISBN: 1–57505–624–0 (lib. bdg. : alk. paper)
    ISBN: 1–57505–709–3 (pbk. : alk. paper)
    1. Martin Luther King Jr. Day—Juvenile literature. 2. King, Martin Luther, Jr. 1929–1968—Juvenile literature. 3. African Americans—Biography—Juvenile literature. 4. Baptists—United States—Clergy—Biography—Juvenile literature. 5. African Americans—Civil rights—History—20th century—Juvenile literature. [1. Martin Luther King Jr. Day. 2. King, Martin Luther, Jr. 1929–1968. 3. Civil rights workers. 4. Clergy. 5. African Americans—Biography. 6. Holidays.] I. Mitchell, Hetty, ill. II. Lowery, Linda. Martin Luther King Day. III. Title. IV. Series.
    E185.97.K5L69 2004
    323'.092—dc21   2003000158

Manufactured in the United States of America
  2 3 4 5 6 – JR – 09 08 07 06 05 04

To children everywhere—
May they have the freedom to dream
and the courage to live their dreams

Author's note

Martin Luther King Jr. loved to learn "big words" when he was a boy. As he grew older, he was able to use these words to explain the ideas he believed in. Here are some important words that Dr. King used.

Laws are made to protect our **civil rights**. Those are the rights of all people to enjoy life, freedom, and equal treatment. When a law takes away someone's civil rights and does not protect everyone equally, it is an **unjust law**. When people try to change any unjust condition, they have a choice of taking **peaceful action** or using **violence**. Violence causes hurt to others and damage to property. Dr. King showed people that peaceful action solves problems better than violence does. Talking honestly about problems, marching to make others aware of unjust conditions, and voting for leaders who want to change unjust laws are all peaceful ways to work for change.

We can create change in our own lives by understanding the meaning of these words. Like Dr. King, we can treat others in a just manner and make our homes and our world better by using peaceful action to solve our problems. On Martin Luther King Jr. Day—and every day—we can make a difference.

It was Monday, January 20, 1986.

Church bells rang out across America.

There were parades in Chicago

and marches in New York City.

Four hundred people rode a "freedom train" across the state of Washington. Why was everybody celebrating?

Leaders from all over the world
met in Atlanta, Georgia.
They talked about peace and justice.

In Arizona, children let
hundreds of balloons fly up
to fill the sky with color.
People were celebrating from Alaska to
Florida, from Hawaii to Washington, D.C.
Why?
It was the first time Americans had
celebrated Martin Luther King Jr.'s
birthday as a national holiday.
More than 27 countries
across the world celebrated, too.
People talked about how Dr. King had
made the world a better place.
Who was Martin Luther King Jr.?
How did he make the world better?

Martin Luther King Jr. was born on
January 15, 1929.
When he was little, his family
called him "M.L."
He lived with his parents, his sister,
and his brother in a big house
on Auburn Avenue in Atlanta, Georgia.

M.L. felt safe and happy in his home.

Three blocks away was another place

M.L. loved to be.

It was the Ebenezer Baptist Church.

His father was the minister there.

His mother led the choir.

M.L.'s parents had some firm rules
for their family.
No matter what the children were doing,
they *always* had to be home for supper.
Suppertime was important.
It was a time for the whole family
to share their ideas and their feelings.
It was at the dinner table that M.L.'s
father and mother taught him one of the
most important lessons of his life.
They taught him to treat all people
with respect.

WAITING ROOM
White   Passengers only

Not everyone in Atlanta knew how to
treat others with respect.
As M.L. grew older, he saw that
white people and black people
were treated differently.

M.L. and his white friends could not drink from the same water fountains. They could not even use the same public restrooms.

M.L.'s best friend was white.

From the time they could walk,

the two friends had played together

on Auburn Avenue.

Then came their first day of school.

M.L. was sent to a school

for black children.

His friend was sent to a school

with other white children.

After school, M.L. ran

to see his friend.

When he knocked on the door,

his friend's mother said that her son was

too busy to come out and play.

She said he was busy

the next day, too . . . and the next.

M.L and his friend were never allowed

to play together again.

M.L. finally asked his mother
why he could not play
with his best friend.
M.L.'s mother took him onto her lap.
It was because M.L. was black
and his friend was white, she explained.
His friend's parents didn't want their son
to play with a black child.
M.L. did not understand.
He knew that the color of his skin
should not make any difference
to his friend's parents.
M.L.'s mother held him tight.
"You are as good as anyone,"
she told him.

It just did not seem fair to M.L.
When he grew up, he thought, he
would try to change things.

M.L. worked very hard in school.
He had always loved learning the big
words his father used when he preached.

Now was his chance to learn how
to use those big words.
He hoped that someday he could use
powerful words to tell people
about respecting others.
Martin studied so hard that he
started college when he was only 15.

Martin never stopped thinking about how
he could make the world a better place.
He thought about being a doctor and
helping people when they were sick.
He thought about being a lawyer so that
he could help people who were
in trouble with the law.

Finally Martin made up his mind.
He decided to become a preacher,
like his father and his grandfather.

He went to a school for ministers.
It was there that Martin learned about
Mohandas Gandhi.
Gandhi was a man who showed
the people of India peaceful ways to change
the unjust laws of their government.
Gandhi did not use violence.

26

Martin read everything he
could find about Gandhi.
He began to think about ways he could
use his own preaching to teach others
some of Gandhi's ideas.

Martin went to yet another school.

This time it was in Boston.

By studying even more about being a minister, he earned the title of doctor.

Now he was called Dr. King.

While he was living in Boston, he met a woman named Coretta Scott.

They were married on June 18, 1953.

Less than a year later, people from a church in Montgomery, Alabama, asked Dr. King to be their minister.

In Montgomery, black people had been
angry for many years about unjust laws
and unequal treatment.
Dr. King hoped he could help solve
those problems by preaching
about respect and justice.
He and Mrs. King decided
to move to Montgomery.
Soon after they arrived, Dr. King
became more involved in the problems
than he had ever imagined he would.

In Montgomery, black people had to
sit at the back of the bus.
When white people got on
a full bus, black people
had to give them their seats.
It was a law.

On December 1, 1955,
a woman named Rosa Parks got on
a bus after a hard day at work.
She was very tired,
and she was happy to sit down.

The bus driver told Mrs. Parks
to give her seat to a white man.
Mrs. Parks said "No."
She had paid her money to ride the bus.

She wanted to be treated
the same as the white man.
The driver called the police.
They arrested Mrs. Parks.

Many people in Montgomery felt that
Mrs. Parks had not been treated right.
They wanted to change the unjust law.
They asked Dr. King to help them.
Dr. King and other black leaders
worked out a plan.
They asked black people
to stay off the buses so that
the bus company would lose money.

Black people walked or took taxis or rode together in cars to get to work.

Black people would not ride the buses
until the unjust law was changed.
It took a year and a lot of work
from many people, but finally
Dr. King's plan was successful.
The law was changed.
Black people could sit
in any seat on the bus.
There were other laws in some
southern states that kept white people
and black people separate.
Dr. King wanted to change
those laws, too.
He wanted to change the laws
without using violence.
He believed that Americans could make
important changes peacefully.

He went to many cities
to talk to crowds of people.
He said that all people have the right
to equal treatment under the law.
Those rights are called civil rights.

Many people believed in civil rights.
They were willing to work hard to make
sure that everyone had those rights.
Dr. King gave speeches to crowds.
He told the people how to use peaceful
ways to change laws that were not just.

One hot August day in 1963,

people marched in Washington, D.C.

There were people of all colors.

They were old and young, rich and poor.

It was the biggest civil rights

march ever held.

Dr. King stood before the crowd.

"I have a dream today, " he said.

"I have a dream that one day . . . little

black boys and black girls will

be able to join hands with little white

boys and white girls and walk together

as sisters and brothers."

Many Americans also had this dream.

They wanted to help make it come true.

There were some people, though, who
did not agree with Dr. King's words.
They tried to stop him from doing his
work by putting him in jail.
Then he could not talk to crowds.

One winter, someone threw
a bomb at the Kings's house.
Mrs. King ran out with their baby girl.
The explosion just missed them.

At times like this, Dr. King
became sad and discouraged.
He worried about the family he loved.
Sometimes it seemed as if
nobody was listening to his words.
He wondered if he should just stop.
Again and again, he decided
to keep on working for his dream
of equality and justice.

In December 1964, he was given
the Nobel Peace Prize.
It meant that his peaceful work
had been noticed by the world.
Part of the prize was $54,000.
He gave the money to groups of people
who were working for civil rights.

Martin Luther King Jr. continued to work
to solve the problems of black people.

Dr. King also worked to help
poor people gain their rights.
He tried to help all Americans
who were being treated unjustly.

In April 1968, he went to Tennessee
to help a group of garbage workers.
While standing on the balcony outside
his motel room, Dr. King was shot.
People all over the world were
shocked, angry, and sad.

Though Dr. King is now gone,
he left us with his dream.
Dr. King's work was so important that
many people wanted to honor him.
They wanted to celebrate his birthday
as a national holiday.
The United States as a nation has
honored only one other person
in this way—George Washington.
Fifteen years after Dr. King's death,
in 1983, Congress voted to create a
holiday to honor Martin Luther King Jr.
The first celebration would be in 1986.
President Ronald Reagan signed the bill.
The holiday became official.
Dr. King's birthday is January 15.
So on the third Monday of every January,
we celebrate Martin Luther King Jr. Day.

On Martin Luther King Jr. Day, we take time
to remember what Dr. King did to make
our world a better place.
Even more, we try to think of ways that
we can live Dr. King's dream each day.

He dreamed of love, peace, and justice.

He dreamed that we can all work together,

no matter what color our skin is.

He worked hard for his dream.

Now it is our turn.

Important Dates

1929—Martin Luther King Jr. was born on January 15 in Atlanta, Georgia.

1944—Martin began his studies at Morehouse College.

1948—Martin became a minister and began studying at Crozer Theological Seminary.

1951—Martin graduated from Crozer and went to Boston University.

1953—Martin married Coretta Scott.

1954—Martin took a job as a minister in Montgomery, Alabama.

1955—Martin helped lead the bus boycott in Montgomery.

1956—The law changed to say that black people could sit anywhere on city buses, and the bus boycott ended.

1963—Martin gave his famous "I Have a Dream" speech in Washington, D.C.

1964—Martin won the Nobel Peace Prize.

1968—Martin was killed in Memphis, Tennessee.

1983—President Ronald Reagan signed a bill making Martin Luther King Jr. Day a national holiday.

1986—Martin Luther King Jr. Day was celebrated for the first time as a national holiday.

Celebrating Martin Luther King Jr. Day

There are lots of way to remember and honor Dr. King on Martin Luther King Jr. Day. Schools and many businesses close for the day in his memory. People take part in parades, marches, and rallies. Churches and other places of worship host special events. Public spaces such as schools, libraries, and museums host tributes to Martin Luther King Jr. At these tributes, children and adults might sing songs, put on plays, or give speeches. In many cities, people of all ages find ways to volunteer in their community. What will you do the next time you celebrate Martin Luther King Jr. Day?

Websites about Martin Luther King Jr. Day

Celebrate: Holidays in the U.S.A.
<http://www.usis.usemb.se/Holidays/celebrate/mlk.html>

The King Center
<http://www.thekingcenter.org/>

Martin Luther King Jr. Day of Service
<http://www.mlkday.org/>

Thoughts on Martin Luther King Jr.

"I would advise [young Americans] to read, study as much as they can and be concerned enough to think about Dr. King as a man and a leader. As they read and hear, they should . . . try to find in themselves their own places as citizens in the world."

—Mrs. Rosa Parks, civil rights worker

"One needs to try to follow his teachings. If one follows his teachings, then one surely can live the dream."

—Mrs. Coretta Scott King